WVU ISN'T JUST A PLACE.
IT'S AN IDEAL. A SPIRIT. A PROMISE.
YOU'RE A MOUNTAINEER.
AND THIS IS OUR CREED.

As a Mountaineer, I will:

Practice academic and personal integrity,

Value wisdom and culture,

Foster lifetime learning,

Practice civic responsibility and good stewardship,

Respect human dignity and cultural diversity.

In order to become a meaningful member of
West Virginia University and the society in which
I live, I dedicate my energy, my talents and my
intellect to these standards of excellence.

This book belongs to:

....

WVU Class of ....

1867 2017

WHAT IS IT THAT MAKES A MOUNTAINEER?

It's passion, innovation and a strong work ethic. It's a commitment to service, fierce pride and a pioneering spirit. It's something intangible that connects our community — across campus and beyond. It's our traditions. What is it that makes a Mountaineer? You're about to find out.

HOW TO USE THIS BOOK.

Use this book to learn about WVU traditions — and to make your own.

▼ Fill in these boxes with your own memories of WVU traditions and campus experiences.

My favorite classes:

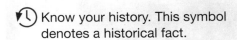

....

....

Photo op! Make sure you get a photo at the place or event where you see this symbol.

🕐 Know your history. This symbol denotes a historical fact.

   As your Mountaineer story unfolds, make sure you share your journey with us! Tweet us, Snap us and tag us on Instagram: WestVirginiaU.

WE ARE DETERMINED TO GO FIRST.

Like the resourceful people who first settled West Virginia's hills, we find creative solutions and blaze trails to new discoveries. #GoFirst

WVU is one of

ONLY 115 INSTITUTIONS

to receive the R1 research status designation out of the 4,500+ schools in the nation.

The world's first institute devoted to the study of

HUMAN MEMORY

is on our campus.

The FBI named WVU its national leader for biometrics research. We house the nation's largest forensic science and

CRIME SCENE TRAINING

complex, and we were the first to offer a bachelor's degree in forensic science.

We are

LISTENING TO THE UNIVERSE.

The National Science Foundation awarded WVU $14.5 million to establish the Physics Frontiers Center to study gravitational waves using the nearby Green Bank Telescope.

WVU researchers raised questions and made

WORLDWIDE HEADLINES

about ethical vehicle emissions testing – and they are one of a handful of groups in the world that could do it.

As one of only 10 labs in the world using large-scale 3-D reconstructions of

BRAIN CELLS,

the Center for Neuroscience is pioneering unprecedented insight into the cellular processes of the brain.

IT'S IN OUR BLOOD, IT'S IN OUR SWEAT AND IT'S IN OUR NATURE.

Serving the state of West Virginia — and the world — is at the core of WVU's mission. The benefits of WVU Extension, healthcare and service programs are seen in every county in the state.

> "West Virginia University is West Virginia's university. Our campus does not end at the borders of Morgantown."
>
> — WVU President E. Gordon Gee

IMPROVING RURAL HEALTH

Before graduation, all Dentistry, Medicine, Nursing and Pharmacy students complete a rural rotation, providing care to patients across the state. Bonnie's Bus, a mobile mammography service, has provided over 13,900 breast cancer screening mammograms throughout West Virginia.

40,000 HOURS

The College of Law provides about 40,000 hours of free legal services and student pro bono projects annually.

EXCEPTIONAL OUTREACH

WVU is among only 6 percent of all universities that have earned the Carnegie Foundation's Community Engagement Classification. With global initiatives like medical and engineering programs in Fiji and 4-H programs in Chile, the impact of WVU's goodwill can be seen well beyond the state's borders.

$1.125 BILLION

Through June 30, 2017, alumni and friends contributed nearly $1.125 billion to A State of Minds: The Campaign for West Virginia's University.

1-IN-5

WVU Extension educators and volunteers guide 1-in-5 (over 80,000) West Virginia youths in "learn by doing" 4-H projects and activities that build citizenship and career skills.

183

Community partners need volunteers, so students always have places to serve.

A (VERY) BRIEF HISTORY.

WVU's history spans 150 years. Here are a few of the big events that have taken place.

1867 West Virginia legislators propose building a new college in the Mountain State, and at the urging of State Sen. William Price, choose Morgantown as the location.

1877 Woodburn Hall (then called New Hall) is completed.

1914 Enrollment exceeds 1,000 and Mining Extension starts, becoming the first program in the nation to train miners.

Coeds enjoy a ride in a convertible in the early 1900s.

1929 A graduate school opens with six fellowship programs.

1933 The Athenaeum, which debuted as a literary magazine in 1887, becomes The Daily Athenaeum newspaper.

1948 Land for the Evansdale campus is purchased, and enrollment exceeds 8,000.

1948 WVU is selected as the site of the state's new medical center.

1959 Jerry West leads the basketball team to the NCAA Championship, where WVU loses to California 71–70.

1963 WVU Press is established, and the first computer — an IBM — is installed on campus.

1970 Anti-war demonstrations block streets in front of the Mountainlair. State Police use tear gas to restore order.

1974 Women are allowed to join the WVU marching band for the first time.

1980 Mountaineer Field (Milan Puskar Stadium) opens.

1988 Ruby Memorial Hospital opens. The football team goes undefeated but loses 34–21 to Notre Dame in the national championship.

2000 WVU is designated a Doctoral/Research University—Extensive by the Carnegie Foundation.

2009 WVU becomes part of a consortium of universities with $465 million in contracts to provide services to the National Energy Technology Laboratory.

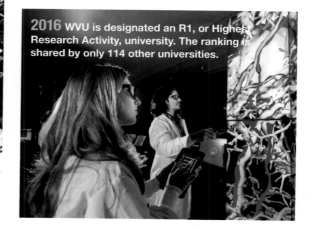

2016 WVU is designated an R1, or Highest Research Activity, university. The ranking is shared by only 114 other universities.

FAMOUS ALUMS

As a graduate of WVU, you will be in some pretty good company. These are some notable graduates.

HARRIET E. LYON
Harriet E. Lyon was WVU's first woman graduate. The only woman in the 14-member Class of 1891, she won the honor of being valedictorian.

CHARLES BROOKE
Charles Frederick Tucker Brooke graduated in 1904 at age 18. He was a member of the first group of Rhodes Scholars from around the world.

JACK HODGE
In 1954, Jack Hodge was the first black undergraduate to receive a degree from WVU, which had immediately desegregated after the Brown v. Board of Education decision.

BARBARA SCHAMBERGER
In 1985, Barbara Schamberger became WVU's first female Rhodes Scholar.

WVU PRESIDENTS

Alexander Martin
1867–1875

John Rhey Thompson
1877–1881

William Lyne Wilson
1882–1883

Eli Marsh Turner
1885–1893

James Goodknight
1895–1897

Jerome Raymond
1897–1901

Daniel Purinton
1901–1911

Thomas Hodges
1911–1914

Frank Trotter
1916–1928

John Turner
1928–1934

Chauncey Boucher
1935–1938

Charles Lawall
1939–1945

Irvin Stewart
1946–1958

Elvis Stahr
1959–1962

Paul Miller
1962–1966

James Harlow
1967–1977

Gene Budig
1977–1981

Harry Heflin
1981

E. Gordon Gee
1981–1985

Diane Reinhard
Interim 1985–1986

Neil Bucklew
1986–1995

David Hardesty
1995–2007

Mike Garrison
2007–2008

Peter McGrath
Interim 2008–2009

James Clements
2009–2013

E.Gordon Gee
2014–present

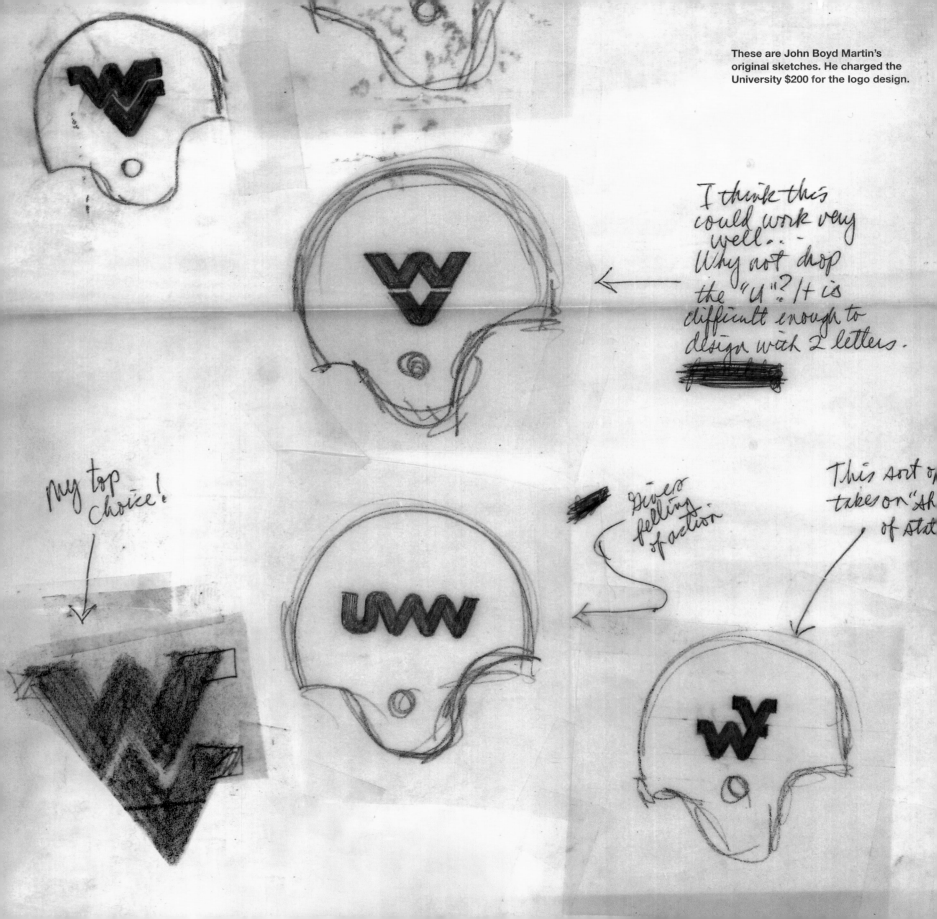

These are John Boyd Martin's original sketches. He charged the University $200 for the logo design.

I think this could work very well... - Why not drop the "U"? It is difficult enough to design with 2 letters.

My top choice!

Gives feeling of action

This sort of takes on "State"

A LOGO LEGEND

Easily one of the most recognizable university logos, WVU's Flying WV was adopted as recently as 1980. WVU Football coach Don Nehlen is often credited with the logo design, but it was actually designer John Boyd Martin's mountain-inspired sketch that became the Flying WV.

Every Mountaineer needs a photo sporting a Flying WV (or two).

SPOTTED

The Flying WV turns up all over the world — and on some big-name celebrities, such as West Virginia natives Jennifer Garner and Brad Paisley.

Most unique place I've seen a Flying WV: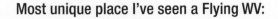

MOUNTAINEER MASCOT

Be sure to get a selfie with the Mountaineer! In addition to attending all major sporting events, the mascot is frequently seen around campus and the community. Follow the mascot on Twitter at @WVUMascot for the latest news.

COONSKIN CAP

BEARD
While male Mountaineers customarily grow a beard during their tenure, it's actually not a requirement for the mascot position.

RIFLE
Preston County native Marvin Wotring has made more than a dozen rifles for WVU's mascots. Each requires about 80 hours of work.

POWDER HORN

BUCKSKINS
Traditionally made from deer hide, the Mountaineer's buckskins are tailored for each mascot.

Since 1934 the buckskin-clad, rifle-toting Mountaineer has been the beloved mascot of WVU. The man or woman selected to represent the mascot is chosen each year by the prestigious senior Mountain Honorary.

Mountaineer mascots when I was a student:

....

....

....

▲ Lawson Hill was the first official Mountaineer.

 —————— 1934 ——————

Rumor has it that the Mountaineer statue in front of the Mountainlair was modeled after NBA legend and WVU graduate Jerry West (although it wasn't). Read more about Jerry West on page 41.

OLD GOLD AND BLUE

SCHOOL COLORS

Students adopted the old gold and blue in 1890. Legend says the idea came from the West Virginia state seal and the first verse of "Hail, West Virginia," the fight song of the University.

▲ Boyd "Slim" Arnold was the first Mountaineer to wear buckskins.

▲ Natalie Tennant was the first female Mountaineer.

1937

1991

STATE OF WEST VIRGINIA.
JUNE 20 1863
★ MONTANI SEMPER LIBERI. ★

RITE OF PASSAGE.

This computer-driven electric car system, called Personal Rapid Transit, has shuttled thousands of WVU students, locals and visitors across town along five stops every day. The annual PRT cram is a long-lived tradition, with students challenged to see how many human bodies will fit in one little gold and blue car — the current record is 97.

Around
83 MILLION PEOPLE
have traveled the PRT since 1975.

Approximately
15,000 PEOPLE
ride the PRT every day during the school year.

The PRT has logged about
22 MILLION MILES
since its opening.

It takes
11.5 MINUTES
to ride the entire length of the PRT system — from the Walnut Street station to the Health Sciences station.

The PRT can travel up to
30 MILES PER HOUR.

Each car can accommodate eight seated passengers and comfortably carry a total of
20 PASSENGERS.

The PRT first began passenger service in 1975, and was built as a government-funded experiment in personal rapid transit systems. Samuel Elias, a WVU Engineering professor, had the idea to bring the experiment to Morgantown.

STAIR MASTER.

West Virginia means hills, people. And hills mean stairs. The most brutal at WVU? Some say it's between the Life Sciences and Business and Economics buildings, with 98 steps (allegedly). Sure the trek is tough, but at least you can skip the treadmill that day.

Most stairs I climbed to get to class:

....

15

Monongahela River

THE HUNT
IS ON.

Grab a friend and go on this scavenger hunt of lesser-known WVU icons.

1 A mast from the Battleship USS West Virginia, damaged during the attack on Pearl Harbor in 1941, stands in Oglebay Plaza.

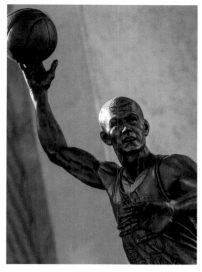

2 Bronze statue of WVU basketball star Jerry West (whose image is the current NBA logo) stands outside the WVU Coliseum. While you're there, visit "Hot Rod" Hundley's statue (pictured here) as well.

3 The little strip of land for pedestrian crossing between the Mountainlair and Martin Hall is known as Grumbein's Island. Urban legend says WVU will pay your tuition if you're hit by a car while crossing — but look out! That's a big myth.

4 The state's largest horse chestnut tree is located 100 feet east of Armstrong Hall.

5 The pylons at the entrance of the Medical Center on the Health Sciences campus have been a symbol of the healing arts for more than 50 years.

6 Legend says students from the agriculture department led a cow up the Woodburn Hall bell tower many years ago and it got stuck and died. That cow is said to haunt the tower, where it can still be heard mooing on certain nights.

7 This 1940s mural in White Hall was replicated for use in a scene in the 2004 "Spiderman 2" film.

8 You'll find a little piece of nature on top of Brooks Hall, where the roof has been partially covered in soil and planted with vegetation as an example of green roof technology.

CAMPUS FASHION.

Late 1800s

Early 1900s

1960s

As early as 1909, freshman males were required to wear "freshman beanies" on and off campus.

1970s

1990s and early 2000s

GET YOUR GEAR.

In Mountaineer Country, WVU gear pops up more places than we can count. But for some of the widest selection on campus, check out the WVU Official Bookstore on University Avenue. From this year's official fan shirt to the perfect gold or blue polo to wear to the Stripe the Stadium football game to the ugliest ugly WVU holiday sweater — you'll find something for every occasion. Or browse a massive selection online at **shopwvu.com**.

My favorite place to get Mountaineer gear:

....

IN THE LIMELIGHT.

WVU inspires greatness. Ignites passions. And fuels amazing futures. Check out a few of the well-known figures who've been drawn to our campuses — as students, faculty and visitors.

DON KNOTTS ▶

Comedian, performer and star of the "Andy Griffith Show," Don Knotts is still known as one of the greatest TV actors of all time. Born in Morgantown, Knotts attended WVU after returning from the service in WWII. He graduated in 1948 and returned many times to share his talents and wisdom with the next generation.

DAN CARDER

WVU engineer Dan Carder, who led the research team that broke open the Volkswagen emissions scandal, was named to the 2016 Time 100, the magazine's annual list of the 100 most influential people in the world.

JOHN RUSSO ▶

John Russo's brilliant — and perhaps twisted — imagination laid the foundation for some of our most iconic horror films. As co-author of the 1968 film "Night of the Living Dead," Russo dreamed up the first zombies to ever grace the silver screen. A 1961 graduate of WVU, Russo has since written, produced or directed more than 20 films and authored more than 20 books.

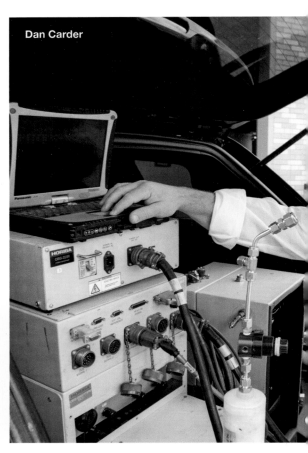

Dan Carder

Margie Mason

◄ MUHAMMAD ALI

Boxing champion and anti-war activist Muhammad Ali, also known as Cassius Clay, toured universities across the country speaking out against the Vietnam War. He stopped in Morgantown in 1969 at the behest of WVU students and spoke in the Mountainlair ballroom during the Festival of Ideas.

BLANCHE LAZZELL

A native of West Virginia, Blanche Lazzell matriculated into West Virginia University in 1901 to study fine art. She would go on to become a pioneering early modernist and abstract painter, printmaker and designer known especially for her woodcuts.

◄ KATHERINE JOHNSON

Physicist, NASA scientist and mathematician, Katherine Johnson was not only the first African American woman to attend WVU's graduate school in 1938, but went on to contribute to the United States' aeronautics and space programs. She helped calculate the trajectory for Project Mercury and the 1969 Apollo 11 flight to the Moon.

TINA TURNER

On November 20, 1985, Tina Turner set her sights on Morgantown and delivered a killer performance in the WVU Coliseum. Her tour helped solidify her status as a major solo artist and live performer.

MARGIE MASON

Margie Mason and three AP colleagues earned the Pulitzer Prize Gold Medal for Public Service in 2016 for their 18-month investigation of slavery and severe labor abuses in Southeast Asia. As a result of their work, more than 2,000 slaves were freed.

HOME SWEET HOME.

Our students live in 12 residence halls and four apartment complexes with everything from private balconies to on-site fitness rooms to fully immersive living-learning communities. Every residence hall and apartment complex has a culture and a focus, where students can live independently or take part in group programming like camping, volunteering and tours of nearby cities.

In 1867, tuition for a 13-week term was $8.00. Room and board was $3.50 per week. The average student would have paid between $187.50 and $249.00 for a full academic year.

WVU opened its first residence hall in 1919 — Woman's Hall (now Stalnaker Hall, named for a longtime professor of psychology, Elizabeth Mattingly Stalnaker).

In the 1910s, most WVU students continued to live in boarding houses, sometimes sleeping (rooming) in one house and eating (boarding) in another; thus, like today, they had to pay for room and board. WVU required that the owners or operators of the boarding houses enforce certain regulations for female students, including curfews that prohibited women from staying out too late at night.

The first two Towers of the Evansdale Residential Complex opened in 1965 and the last two Towers in 1968 as baby boomers entered college.

Be sure to take a photo of your room — and with your roommate.

My hall freshman year:

....

STUDENT ORGS

You'll find over 460+ student organizations at WVU. That's 460+ chances to make awesome memories, boost your résumé, meet lifelong friends and maybe even learn something. Gasp. Here are just a handful.

LEND A HAND
WVU has its own Habitat for Humanity organization that believes everyone, everywhere should have a healthy, affordable home. Student volunteers work on various construction and service projects to help give back to the community.

CALLING ALL MANIACS
The Mountaineer Maniacs organization is the largest student org on campus and the premiere student group for Mountaineer athletics. They are the official student section for WVU sports, supporting all athletic teams and promoting good sportsmanship, pride and tradition.

Student orgs I joined:

....

....

....

ACCIO FUN
You don't have to love Harry Potter to get into the spirit of this high-speed, coed contact sport, described as a mixture of rugby, dodgeball and tag. WVU's team started in the Honors Residence Hall in 2010 and became an official student organization in 2012. In 2013, the WVU Quidditch Club became an official U.S. Quidditch and International Quidditch Association member.

GREEK LIFE

With more than 100 years of history on campus, the Greek community is founded on the ideals of scholarship, leadership, friendship and service. The focus on service is only getting bigger with events like the BIG! Greek Day of Service kicking off Greek Week, the annual celebration of Greek culture on campus.

BY THE NUMBERS

3
Greek leadership councils

30
chapters

2,200
students

FALL

From football to Mountaineer Week to Homecoming, fall at WVU is all about Mountaineer pride. The natural beauty of campus and beyond is on full display as the leaves change and fill the mountains with color.

Fall Bucket List:

☐ Attend FallFest.

☐ Stock up on your Mountaineer gear.

☐ Attend a WVU football game. Get a pepperoni roll.

☐ See the The Pride of West Virginia perform.

☐ Enjoy the view from Coopers Rock.

☐ Join a student org.

☐ Watch the Homecoming Parade on High Street.

☐ Cram the PRT during Mountaineer Week (and try the kettle corn).

WELCOME WEEK

One of WVU's biggest — and best — traditions is quite literally an annual celebration of students descending on Morgantown for the start of fall semester. This week of nonstop events and experiences is meant to foster a strong academic and cultural connection to campus among some 5,000 new students and 24,000 returning students. During this week students get acclimated to campus, learn more about academics, volunteer in the community, go on adventures and make friends through activities like cookouts, lawn games, team trivia, bumper cars, yoga and a massive food festival and concert.

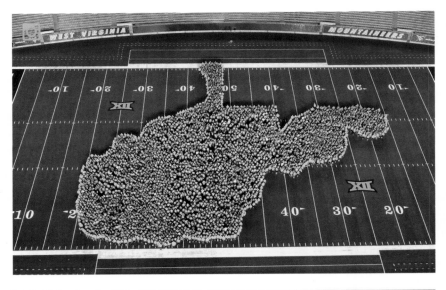

FALLFEST

FallFest is WVU's official welcome to students at the beginning of each fall semester. The concert's lineup isn't announced until a few days before the event, leading to lots of speculation and excitement over who will appear.

29

FOOTBALL

KNOW YOUR EERS. CONFERENCE: Big 12 // FIRST YEAR OF FOOTBALL: 1891 // CURRENT RECORD: 737-485-45 INCLUDES 2016 SEASON

Before becoming the Mountaineers in 1905, WVU was "The Snakes."

At WVU, fall is inseparable from football — it's said that the population of Morgantown more than doubles on game days. So head to the stadium and see what it's all about!

TICKET FROM THE FIRST WVU FOOTBALL GAME I ATTENDED AS A STUDENT

Not into American football? Head over to Dick Dlesk Soccer Stadium and cheer on our Division I women's soccer team — they won the Big 12 Championship and were the national runner-up last year.

LET'S GO ...
MOUNTAINEERS!

A rousing cheer at WVU athletic events led by the Mountaineer cheerleaders and mascot. One side of the stadium chants "Let's Go" and the other side responds "Mountaineers."

FIRST DOWN CHEER

Traditionally sung during football games before the announcement of a first down, fans raise their hands and cheer in unison until the first down call is made. After the call, fans lift their arms up-and-down three times, clap and chant "W-V-U! First down!"

BACKYARD BRAWL

For more than a century, WVU's famous annual football and basketball games against the University of Pittsburgh were called "The Backyard Brawl." Back by popular demand, the Brawl will return with a scheduled four-game series from 2022 to 2025.

Mountaineer Field was located Downtown — where the Life Sciences Building and College of Business and Economics are now — from 1924 to 1987.

THE PRIDE OF WV

The WVU Marching Band, also called "The Pride of West Virginia," is an award-winning, 330-plus member marching band known for goose-bumps-inducing performances and exciting visuals.

PREGAME PLAYLIST

FIGHT MOUNTAINEERS
One of WVU's two fight songs, "Fight Mountaineers" begins with the chant of "W… V … U … WVU!"

MOUNTAIN DEW
Traditional tune that you'll come to love.

SIMPLE GIFTS
A traditional Shaker song.

ALMA MATER
The Alma Mater will pull at your heartstrings. Listen to the choral version for a real treat.

NATIONAL ANTHEM
You know this one.

COUNTRY ROADS
It's the ultimate WVU tradition. You'll hear it at games. You'll hear it at events. Heck, you'll hear random people belting it in the streets. It's impossible not to join in. Trust us.

HAIL, WEST VIRGINIA!
WVU's other fight song ends the pregame show and brings on the football team.

Favorite song performed by The Pride of West Virginia:

The WVU Marching Band was formed in 1901 as an all-male ROTC Band and had eight members.

In 2016, the band performed in the Macy's Thanksgiving Day Parade.

COUNTRY ROADS

You'll hear it everywhere in West Virginia — from weddings to restaurants to athletic events. "Take Me Home, Country Roads" by John Denver has been performed at every home football pregame show since 1972 and after every home win.

Almost heaven, West Virginia
Blue ridge mountains, Shenandoah river
Life is old there, older than the trees
Younger than the mountains, growin' like a breeze

Country roads, take me home
To the place I belong
West Virginia, mountain momma
Take me home, country roads

All my memories, gathered round her
Miner's lady, stranger to blue water
Dark and dusty, painted on the sky
Misty taste of moonshine, teardrops in my eyes

Country roads, take me home
To the place I belong
West Virginia, mountain momma
Take me home, country roads

I hear her voice in the mornin' hour she calls me
The radio reminds me of my home far away
And drivin' down the road I get a feeling
That I should have been home yesterday, yesterday

Country roads, take me home
To the place I belong
West Virginia, mountain momma
Take me home, country roads

Country roads, take me home
To the place I belong
West Virginia, mountain momma,
Take me home, country roads
Take me home, country roads
Take me home, country roads

You'll find yourself arm-in-arm with your neighbor, swaying back and forth as you sing "Country Roads" many times as a student — and long after you graduate.

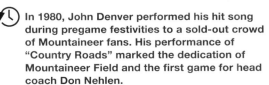

In 1980, John Denver performed his hit song during pregame festivities to a sold-out crowd of Mountaineer fans. His performance of "Country Roads" marked the dedication of Mountaineer Field and the first game for head coach Don Nehlen.

In 2014, Brad Paisley surprised fans with a pregame performance of "Country Roads" at the WVU vs. Maryland game.

HOMECOMING

Since 1910 every fall during a home football game weekend, alumni, students and the community come together for festivities across campus and Morgantown.

The 1969 Homecoming Parade

MOUNTAINEER WEEK

The University created this event in 1947 to promote school spirit. It started as a weekend event. By 1972, it had stretched to a weeklong celebration packed with concerts, food and fun.

MR. AND MRS. MOUNTAINEER
Since 1958, during the first home football game of Mountaineer Week, two individuals with true Mountaineer Spirit, excellent academic records and a full load of extracurricular activities have been chosen to represent the University. The designation remains one of WVU's biggest honors.

MOUNTAINEER WEEK EVENTS AND AWARDS

ARTISAN CRAFT FAIR AND QUILT SHOW
Check out traditional Appalachian crafts in the Mountainlair ballroom.

FAMILY FUN DAY
Families are invited to participate in activities related to Appalachian heritage.

FIDDLE CONTEST
An Appalachian-style old-time fiddle contest.

MOST LOYALS
Faculty, staff and alumni are rewarded for their loyalty and service.

MOUNTAINEER IDOL
WVU's take on "American Idol" is a chance to stretch your vocal cords, or just listen.

PRT CRAM
Every year during Mountaineer Week students test the limits of the PRT's capacity, lining up to squeeze into a car set up in front of the Mountainlair. The year 2000 set the record with 97 students.

PRT Cram record when
I was a student:

....

WINTER

Winter may be chilly here in Morgantown, but a beautiful snowfall will make it worth the shivers. If you really can't take the cold, head inside to a basketball game or a performance at the Creative Arts Center.

Winter Bucket List:

☐ Ice skate behind the Lair.

☐ Watch a basketball game from the student section.

☐ Find a cozy study spot (hint: the Reading Room at the Downtown Library is a favorite).

☐ See a performance at the Creative Arts Center.

☐ Snow day!

☐ Attend a lecture during the Festival of Ideas.

☐ Venture off campus for skiing or snowboarding.

☐ Head over to the WVU Rifle Range near the Coliseum and cheer on one the best rifle teams in the country — they have won the national championship 19 times.

FESTIVAL OF IDEAS

Every year WVU welcomes thought leaders and public figures to Morgantown during the yearlong Festival of Ideas, a speaker series that has been free and open to the public since its revival in 1995 by WVU President Emeritus David C. Hardesty, Jr. Get ready to expand your mind listening to talks by everyone from NBA and Mountaineer basketball star Jerry West to Nelson Mandela's grandson, Ndaba Mandela.

Arianna Huffington — co-founder of The Huffington Post — came to campus in 2008.

In 2013, Newark, New Jersey, mayor Cory Booker spoke about the strengths and challenges of diversity in America.

Jerry West spoke at WVU in 2011 about his autobiography "West by West: My Charmed, Tormented Life."

Best speakers I saw at WVU:

....

....

....

PERFORMANCES

For a city of less than 100,000 people — students included — Morgantown has hosted some incredible entertainers, theatrical performances and singers. And WVU Arts & Entertainment, a division of Student Life, is at the heart of it all. Performers from Tina Turner to Whoopi Goldberg to Drake have played the Coliseum or the Creative Arts Center.

Built in 1970, the domed Coliseum is one of the University's most-recognized buildings, and home court for WVU basketball.

BASKETBALL

Step foot in the 14,000-seat Coliseum and you'll immediately see — and hear — why it's known as one of the toughest college basketball environments. Get there early for a spot in the courtside student section.

TICKET FROM THE FIRST WVU BASKETBALL GAME I ATTENDED AS A STUDENT

ROLL OUT THE CARPET

From 1955 to the late 1960s, Mountaineer men's basketball players entered pregame warm-ups on an elaborate gold and blue carpet and practiced with a gold and blue ball. Former Mountaineer basketball player Gale Catlett reintroduced the carpet when he returned as head coach in 1978, and it has since become a highlight.

HIGHLIGHT REEL

Jerry West played in the NBA for the Los Angeles Lakers and was the inspiration for the NBA logo.

Rod "Hot Rod" Hundley was known as the "Clown Prince" of college basketball and went on to broadcast NBA games in the 1970s and 1980s.

In December of 1984, Georgeann Wells became the first woman to dunk a basketball in an NCAA game.

Affectionately known as "Huggy Bear," Bob Huggins is one of the winningest basketball coaches of all time with over 800 victories.

KNOW THYSELF, MOUNTAINEER.

From art to natural history to coalfield artifacts — WVU has repositories of knowledge and culture for every taste.

COOK-HAYMAN PHARMACY MUSEUM

The history of pharmaceuticals is on display in the WVU School of Pharmacy's Cook-Hayman Pharmacy Museum, where you'll find a replicated apothecary's office complete with exhibits of herbal and chemical prescriptions, scales, mortars and pestles, and records from the WVU School of Pharmacy now more than 100 years old. **pharmacy.hsc.wvu.edu**

ART MUSEUM OF WVU

Located near the Creative Arts Center, the Art Museum is a brand-new 5,400-square-foot facility with a collection of more than 3,000 pieces, including international work from as far away as Africa, as well as West Virginian and Appalachian art from greats like Blanche Lazzell. **artmuseum.wvu.edu**

DONALD J. BROHARD HALL OF TRADITIONS

This hall of exhibits at Mylan Puskar Stadium is the ultimate Mountaineer football fan's mecca, with interactive footage of the Mountaineer Marching Band, the Mountaineer mascot and the football program from 1891 to present day on display. Fans can view everything from bowl trophies to helmets, championship rings and jerseys worn by WVU legends.

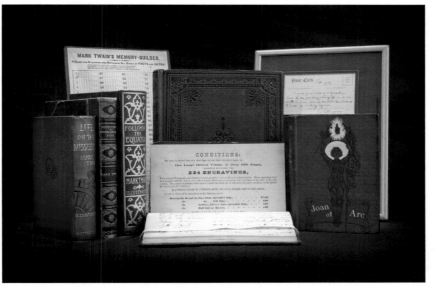

ROYCE J. AND CAROLINE B. WATTS MUSEUM

Visit the Royce J. and Caroline B. Watts Museum on the ground floor of WVU's Mineral Resources Building and you'll find yourself drawn into the history and culture of the state's mining and petroleum industry — where artifacts like rescue equipment, lamps and even canary cages paint a picture of the brave, pioneering men and women who risked their lives to bring minerals to the world.
wattsmuseum.wvu.edu

WVU SCHOOL OF NATURAL RESOURCES' NATURAL HISTORY MUSEUM

Created in 2008, the WVU Natural History Museum can be found in Percival Hall on the Evansdale campus. Here, hundreds of preserved animals from around the world — some now rare or extinct — as well as their natural histories are on display.

WVU LIBRARIES WEST VIRGINIA AND REGIONAL HISTORY CENTER

Although the West Virginia and Regional History Center's main mission is to collect, preserve and provide public access to books and artifacts from the state and region, the center also houses the state's premier collection of rare books — some from as far back as the 1300s. With Shakespeare's Four Folios, first editions of Jane Austen's and Mark Twain's novels and more, the center beckons bibliophiles.

My favorite WVU museum:

....

SPRING

Sure, finals and graduations are looming. But WVU and the greater Morgantown area have a full roster of fairs, festivals and events to distract even the best students from spring cram season. You can grab a seat at the baseball stadium and root for the home team, go on a guided spring wildflower walk at the Core Arboretum or take in a performance from acts like the Blue Man Group and the Harlem Globetrotters. Off campus you'll find everything from Irish road bowling to the Mountain Film Festival to an entire day devoted to the love — and unabashed sampling — of chocolate.

Spring Bucket List:

☐ Watch a baseball game at the new ballpark.

☐ Spring break!

☐ Have a study session on the Mountainlair green or Woodburn lawn.

☐ Relax before finals with a free massage during Fun Before Finals.

☐ Eat a Flying WV cookie. They're everywhere around graduation.

☐ Have a picnic at one of Morgantown's many parks.

GREEN GETAWAYS.

Get lost — but not really — in one of Morgantown's green spaces.

Coopers Rock State Park

WEST VIRGINIA BOTANIC GARDEN

What was once a reservoir off Tyrone Road is now an 82-acre space that includes landscaped gardens and stately trees with shimmering pools. Sign up for a morning yoga in the garden session or learn how to take killer nature photos.
1061 Tyrone Road

KREPPS PARK

Part of Morgantown's extensive park system, Krepps is a 36-acre parcel with wooded trails, an outdoor swimming pool with a children's aquatic area, a pavilion, picnic areas and a dog park.
1235 Parkview Drive

COOPERS ROCK STATE FOREST

One of the most sweeping — and selfied — views in the state is just outside the city limits off I-68. But don't just stop at the overlook. Pull on your hiking boots and explore 12,713 acres of wild and wonderful.
Coopers Rock Road, Bruceton Mills

◄ WVU CORE ARBORETUM

This 91-acre tract of forested hillside and bottomland near the WVU Coliseum and the Monongahela River is an oasis for visitors from dawn to dusk, with 200-year-old trees and a connection to the area's extensive rail-trail system.
Monongahela Boulevard

My favorite green getaway:

....

BASEBALL

Morgantown's new $121 million, 2,500-seat baseball stadium — complete with a fan store, plenty of concession options and promotions like fireworks and discount ticket days — lies just across the river from Downtown. The Monongalia County Ballpark hosts both the University's Big 12 baseball team and the West Virginia Black Bears minor league team.

There's a reason baseball has been called America's favorite pastime for generations. The crack of the bat, the smell of popcorn and the roar of the crowd — it's ingrained in our collective imaginations.

Morgantown now has its own minor league team, the West Virginia Black Bears, an affiliate of the Pittsburgh Pirates.

TICKET FROM THE
FIRST BASEBALL GAME I
ATTENDED AS A STUDENT

With PRT car games, pepperoni roll races, giveaways, local foods and drinks and fireworks, baseball in Morgantown is an experience in itself.

DECODE YOUR (OR YOUR STUDENT'S) STUDY STYLE.

Whether you need absolute quiet, a constant caffeine drip or a comfy chair, WVU has an inspiring space for every studious personality. Answer these questions and we'll match you to one of our favorites.

On Friday night before a big test, you can find me:
A. Getting inspired at a poetry reading.
B. Studying until I pass out on my books.
C. Hanging out with friends at a local coffee shop.
D. Curled up with a good book and some chocolate.
E. Heading up an event for the student organization I started.
F. Going to WVUp All Night — all night.

My go-to lunch before an exam is:
A. California roll — those Omega-3s keep me sharp.
B. Anything I can eat with one hand while studying.
C. Coffee — food is secondary.
D. Mac and cheese. Fried chicken. Cheeseburger. It's all about comfort food.
E. Panini I made myself at home.
F. Large pizza, extra cheese. Enough to share.

My Finals Week de-stressor is:
A. Meditation and a bit of hot yoga.
B. De-stress?! Talk to me after this week.
C. Decaf with soy milk. Hold the sugar.
D. Chocolate chip cookies and milk.
E. Stress makes me more productive.
F. No-holds-barred cornhole competition with a few friends.

To really concentrate, I need:
A. A totally Zen atmosphere.
B. Quiet. Complete and utter quiet. Don't even breathe loudly.
C. A double shot of espresso.
D. Something sweet to snack on and a comfy chair.
E. Deadlines. Competition. The possibility of awards or honors.
F. Frequent breaks to chill with my BFF.

Final grades are in, I got:
A. A few Bs, a few A's — in my creative classes.
B. I can't even look. It's too soon.
C. My hands are shaking too much to check right now.
D. I could have done better if the exam room had more comfortable chairs.
E. All A's, of course.
F. Mostly Bs. Same as all of my friends.

More A's. Room to reflect.
Reflection Room, Room G44, Evansdale Library
A quiet, meditative space designed to inspire. You can't actually study here. But you can prepare your mind for optimal studiousness.

More Bs. Deep quiet.
Robinson Reading Room, Wise Library, Downtown
Deep quiet zone in a historic (but not overly distracting) space with thousands of books, articles and online resources at your fingertips. Relax. You'll do fine.

More Cs or a mixture. Coffee shop connoisseur.
Eliza's Coffee Shop, Fourth Floor Downtown Library
Grab a seat before it fills up. Eliza's — a coffee shop and study space with food, a fun reading selection, daily newspapers and computers — is a student favorite just a few steps from all the resources of the Downtown Library.

More Ds. Comfort king.
Vandalia Lounge, Mountainlair, Downtown
A place to study or even catch some z's with plush chairs, a fireplace and a great food selection nearby.

More Es. Type-A+.
Scholars Lounge, Mountainlair, Downtown
Quiet and inspiring, with plaques on the walls honoring WVU's Truman, USA Today and other award-winning scholars. Something to aspire to.

More Fs. Group studier.
Fifth Floor, Evansdale Crossing, Evansdale
Drag your friends to the "living room," a fun place to meet, eat, study, hang out between classes and chat it up into the evening.

THE DA

For 128 years the Daily Athenaeum, WVU's editorially independent, student-run newspaper, has been the go-to news source for the University community and Morgantown. Students produce the newspaper, its website and its social media while gaining skills that help them land prestigious internships and jobs. It's a fun community open to all students and all majors.

thedaonline.com

The Daily Athenaeum was

STARTED IN 1888.

The newspaper is

DISTRIBUTED TO 260 LOCATIONS.

Check them out online at thedaonline.com.

My favorite place to study:

....

"Life passes quickly enough as it is ... there's enough adversity as is. It will be over before you know it. You need to make the most of it."

– former President Bill Clinton, WVU commencement 2010

COMMENCEMENT

Commencement at WVU is bittersweet. Thousands of students say goodbye to the old gold and blue every year and hello to fulfilling careers all over the world. Most take their tear-filled photos in front of Woodburn, or drag their friends to Coopers Rock for one more picnic on top of the world, but hardly anyone leaves without experiencing a proper send-off at — you guessed it — the Mountaineer Send-Off, an event complete with free food, giveaways, music, photos and fun.

WVU SEAL

WVU's seal was designed by its first president, Reverend Alexander Martin, and adopted in 1869. The Greek means: "Add to your faith virtue and to virtue knowledge" (from the King James Bible). The outer Latin reads: "Seal of the West Virginia University Established 7 February 1867." The seal appears on every WVU diploma.

NOTABLE SPEAKERS

Won't you be my neighbor? Mr. Rogers spoke to 1995 graduates in the same tone he had during their childhood — but with a powerful message.

Homer Hickam, "Rocket Boys" author, connected with students when he spoke to the class of 1999.

Cisco CEO John Chambers got up close and personal in the 2001 graduation ceremony — walking with a cordless microphone and engaging individual students.

"Find what you love and figure out how to get paid for it."

– "Today" show host Hoda Kotb, WVU commencement 2009

MONTICOLA 1919

WVU's student yearbook, the "Monticola," was founded in 1896. Visit go.wvu.edu/monticola to see the digital archive.

CLASS RING

Undergraduates wear it with the logo facing their hearts. During commencement, graduates move the tassel on their caps from left to right and turn their rings so the logo faces outward.

GRADUATE ATTIRE

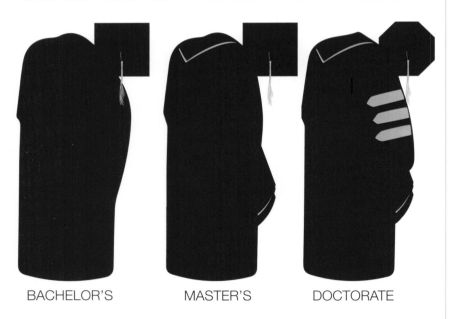

BACHELOR'S   MASTER'S   DOCTORATE

MORTARBOARD/TAM

The head covering of the modern academic costume was developed from the skullcap worn by the clergy in cold weather to protect their bare heads. In universities, this skullcap acquired a point on top, which gradually evolved into a tassel.

HOOD

The modern hood is colored according to the scholarly field of the individual and bears, on the inner liner, the official colors of the institution that conferred the graduate's degree.

ROBES

Long, flowing robes date back to the Middle Ages, when they were used for warmth in unheated buildings. The attire helped distinguish academics and became tradition.

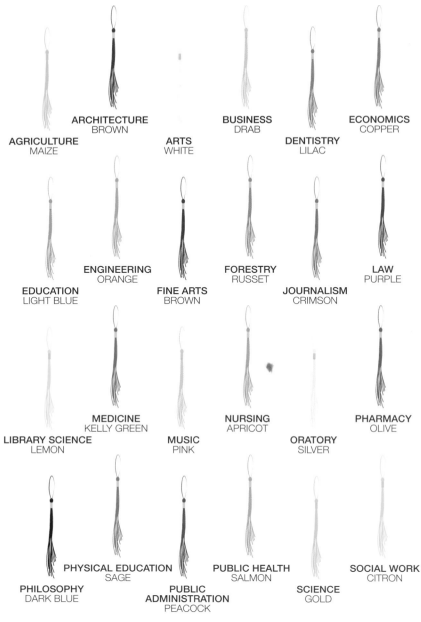

AGRICULTURE
MAIZE

ARCHITECTURE
BROWN

ARTS
WHITE

BUSINESS
DRAB

DENTISTRY
LILAC

ECONOMICS
COPPER

EDUCATION
LIGHT BLUE

ENGINEERING
ORANGE

FINE ARTS
BROWN

FORESTRY
RUSSET

JOURNALISM
CRIMSON

LAW
PURPLE

LIBRARY SCIENCE
LEMON

MEDICINE
KELLY GREEN

MUSIC
PINK

NURSING
APRICOT

ORATORY
SILVER

PHARMACY
OLIVE

PHILOSOPHY
DARK BLUE

PHYSICAL EDUCATION
SAGE

PUBLIC
ADMINISTRATION
PEACOCK

PUBLIC HEALTH
SALMON

SCIENCE
GOLD

SOCIAL WORK
CITRON

GRADUATION CAPS

Sequins. Glitter pens. Felt letters. That's the view from above during any WVU commencement ceremony. Students have been decorating their mortarboards for years with notes of future aspirations, gold-and-blue embellishments or the ever-popular Flying WV.

FLYING WV COOKIES

This shortbread treat, cut in the shape of the University logo and decorated with gold and blue icing, is perhaps our most delicious branded item. But its origin is a bit of a mystery. Sometime in the 1980s or 90s, WVU head baker Nancy Ruckle came up with the top secret recipe. And it has remained under lock and key ever since.

POMP AND CIRCUMSTANCE

Duuuuh-dun-dun-dun-duuuuh-dun. The familiar marching tune "Pomp and Circumstance" narrates nearly every graduation ceremony. The processional, composed by Sir Edward Elgar, became associated with graduations in 1905 — the year Elgar received an honorary doctorate from Yale University. His tune, which was used for the coronation of King Edward VII, was played as a recessional at the ceremony. Other universities followed suit — Princeton, University of Chicago, Columbia — until it became the song that all students hear at graduation.

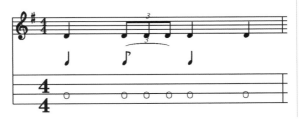

MACE

The ornamental staff is brought to the platform by the grand marshal, who taps it three times and places it in a designated holder to signify the beginning of the ceremony. The mace was handcrafted by a WVU professor.

WEST VIRGINIA SUGAR COOKIES

No, we aren't giving away the coveted Flying WV cookie recipe. But this one is pretty darn close.

COOKIES

1/2 cup unsalted butter at room temp
2/3 cup granulated sugar
2 1/3 cup all-purpose flour
2 large eggs
1 tablespoon pure vanilla extract
1 teaspoon salt

ICING

1 cup confectioner's sugar
1 tablespoon milk
1 tablespoon light corn syrup
1 drop fresh lemon juice
 colored sugar or sprinkles, to taste

In a bowl, cream the butter and sugar until light and fluffy. Beat in the eggs and vanilla.

Slowly add flour and mix till just combined. Wrap dough in plastic wrap and chill for at least 30 minutes.

Preheat oven to 350 degrees Fahrenheit.

Roll out dough and cut into shapes with cookie cutters or a knife. Bake on a sheet pan or a parchment lined sheet pan for 10 to 15 minutes depending on the size of the cookie. Cookies will be light brown on edges.

Remove cookies to a rack to cool completely.

To make the icing, first sift the confectioner's sugar to remove lumps. Add the milk, corn syrup and lemon juice to the sifted sugar and mix until a smooth, even consistency is achieved. Spread or pipe icing onto cookies. Allow to set for a few minutes until icing has a tacky surface. Use stencils to create your design before icing hardens.

Yield: about 24 cookies

SUMMER

If you're lucky enough to be in Morgantown for the summer — taking classes or just hanging out — don't just sit at home. Sign up in the Study Abroad Office in advance and go on a life-changing international experience in one of 50 countries — from Fiji to Belize to New Zealand. You can even apply for an internship in London or a semester exchange program. In town, grab a friend and feel the burn on the Deckers Creek Half Marathon or the Jim Dunn Memorial 5 Miler, don your leather vest and get ready for one of the largest motorcycle rallies in the region during Mountainfest or take in a play at the West Virginia Public Theater.

Summer Bucket List:

☐ Boat, paddle or swim at Cheat Lake.

☐ Have a West Virginia-style hot dog — slaw and all.

☐ Take a summer class.

☐ Get out of town! Take a road trip around the state or sign up for an international experience.

☐ Catch a women's volleyball game at the Coliseum or a soccer game — both men's and women's teams play in August.

OH, THE PLACES YOU SHOULD GO.

Your college experience doesn't end in the classroom. Or on High Street. Take a weekend — or more — to explore a few highlights of the Mountain State.

● COOPERS ROCK
Hike, bike, camp, rock climb or take a picnic and snap some selfies at one of the most photographed scenic overlooks in the region. (20-minute drive)

● TRANS-ALLEGHENY LUNATIC ASYLUM
Go on a ghost hunt at this allegedly haunted former mental hospital from the 19th century. It's been toured by Syfy's "Ghost Hunters" and the Travel Channel's "Ghost Adventures." You can even spend the night. If you dare. (1-hour drive)

● INDEPENDENCE HALL IN WHEELING
Visit the place where West Virginia was born, absorb the state's unique Civil War history, then do lunch at Later Alligator in town. Ever heard of crepes? You can thank us later. (1-hour, 18-minute drive)

● BLACKWATER FALLS
Getting to Blackwater Falls, a 60-foot cascade at the end of an 8-mile wilderness gorge, is a surprisingly easy trek. And the pictures will look epic. (1-hour, 45-minute drive)

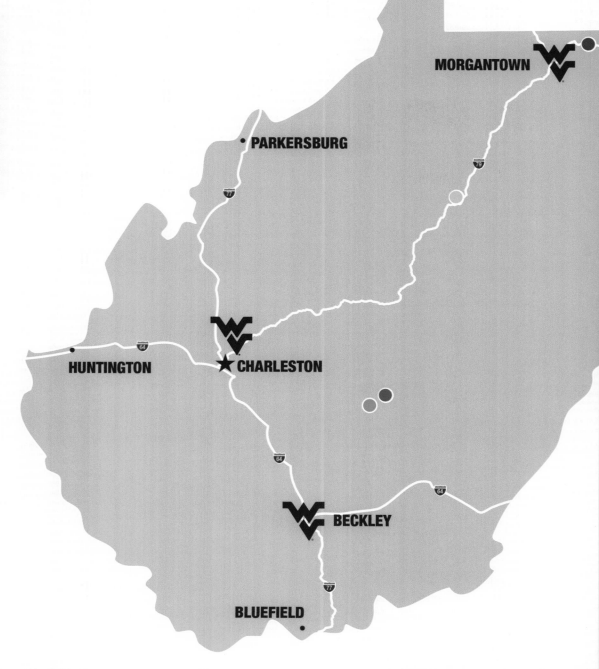

WHEELING

MORGANTOWN

PARKERSBURG

HUNTINGTON

★ CHARLESTON

BECKLEY

BLUEFIELD

My favorite place in the Mountain State:

....

KEYSER
MARTINSBURG

CALL OF THE WILD AND WONDERFUL.

Start your own adventure at the Student Rec Center's Outdoor Recreation Center, where you'll find everything you need for rent. Prices range from $.50 to $15 per day.

RENTABLE EQUIPMENT

Backpacks	Backpacking Stoves	Splash Tops
Bicycles and Helmets	Camp Stoves	Downhill Ski Packages
Bike Racks	Pot Sets	Snowboard Packages
Child's Ride-Behind Bike	3- to 6-Person Tents	Cross-Country Ski Package
Child's Carrier/Trailer	Tarps	Snowshoes
Rock Climbing Shoes and Bouldering Pads	Canoes, Paddles and Carriers	
Sleeping Bags and Sleeping Pads (for all seasons)	Kayaks	
	Dry Bags	
	Wet Suits and Booties	

● **SUMMERSVILLE LAKE**
Take a dip in West Virginia's largest lake — a 2,700-acre blue gem. Learn to water ski. Fail at skiing. Camp. Burn your marshmallows. Whatever. You'll have fun. (2-hour drive)

● **SENECA ROCKS**
Here lies the only true mountain peak (meaning you can't get there unless you can rock climb) on the East Coast of the United States. And you can hike to the top with minimal gear and only a tiny bit of courage. Believe us. The view is worth it. (2-hour, 15-minute drive)

● **NEW RIVER GORGE BRIDGE**
Cross over one of the oldest river systems in the world (That's right. The new river is actually super old.) on what was once the world's longest single-span arch bridge at 3,030 feet long. With special gear, and a trained guide, you can even cross via the gangplank suspended below the bridge. Not for the faint of heart. (2-hour, 17-minute drive)

ADVENTURE WV

What began as an outdoor orientation program for incoming first-year students now includes everything from an outdoor education center and challenge course to a zip line canopy tour and leadership training.

Where I ventured with Adventure WV:

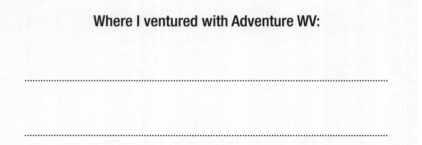

....

....

MORGANTOWN MAINSTAYS

Your seriously unofficial guide to just a few of the best places to eat and hang off campus.

BLACK BEAR BURRITOS
Live music, burritos, quesadillas and dips of all kinds.
132 Pleasant Street; 3119 University Avenue

GENE'S BEER GARDEN
More than just beer, Gene's is a Morgantown institution and the oldest running bar in town. Enjoy live music and, arguably, the best hotdogs in Morgantown.
461 Wilson Avenue

PIZZA AL'S
Good, old fashioned thin-crust pizza with fresh toppings. A student favorite for decades. The large pizza is so big you'll need help getting it out the door.
2952 University Avenue; 1403 Earl L. Core Road; University Town Centre

CHICO BAKERY
West Virginia's official state food — the pepperoni roll — can officially be purchased (hot out of the oven) at this bakery, still made with their famous 1925 recipe.
407 Beechurst Avenue

MARIO'S FISHBOWL
Classic pub fare with a side of history. The original location on Richwood Avenue has been serving its drinks in iconic fishbowl goblets since the 1950s.
704 Richwood Avenue; 3117 University Avenue

WVU ALUMNI ASSOCIATION

Chartered in 1873, the WVU Alumni Association boasts association chapters everywhere from California to Malaysia. Members participate in student recruitment, scholarship fundraising, mentoring, networking — even community service. You can even get involved as a student. The Gold and Blue Crew is a student organization affiliated with the Alumni Association that prepares students for success upon graduation through things like programming, mentorship and events.

The Erickson Alumni Center is the on-campus home of WVU Alumni.

200,000
graduates worldwide

Graduates in
135
nations

Alumni chapters in
29
states

More than
100+
alumni chapters

"IT'S A GREAT DAY TO BE A MOUNTAINEER, WHEREVER YOU MAY BE."

This catchphrase was coined by Tony Caridi, the play-by-play announcer whose familiar voice has been bringing WVU football and basketball games to fans across the nation for decades. Just don't call him "The Voice of the Mountaineers." That title belongs to Jack Fleming exclusively. Fleming was a famous announcer for WVU football and basketball, as well as the Pittsburgh Steelers and Chicago Bulls.

www.mascotbooks.com

WVU Traditions

For more information, please contact:
Mascot Books
620 Herndon Parkway #320
Herndon, VA 20170
info@mascotbooks.com

CPSIA Code: PBANG1217A
ISBN-13: 978-1-68401-148-3

Printed in the United States